HARRINGTON
THROUGH TIME

A Hometown Story

DOUGLAS POORE

AMERICA
THROUGH TIME®
ADDING COLOR TO AMERICAN HISTORY

America Through Time is an imprint of Fonthill Media LLC
www.through-time.com
office@through-time.com

Published by Arcadia Publishing by arrangement with Fonthill Media LLC
For all general information, please contact Arcadia Publishing:
Telephone: 843-853-2070
Fax: 843-853-0044
E-mail: sales@arcadiapublishing.com
For customer service and orders:
Toll-Free 1-888-313-2665

www.arcadiapublishing.com

First published 2019

Copyright © Douglas Poore 2019

ISBN 978-1-63500-093-1

Typeset in Mrs Eaves XL Serif Narrow
Printed and bound in England

INTRODUCTION

"What's in a name?" is a quote from *Romeo and Juliet*, written by William Shakespeare. As in the famous play, a name invokes so much more than the sum of its letters. This is true of anyone's hometown. Our hometown's name recalls our days as children, playing in the park with friends. Some remain, while others are long gone. It reminds us of family, the people that formed us, loved us, and gave us life. Those long-ago holidays, dinners, and memories all shaped who we are. They form a tapestry. Pull on one string and you unravel the story of you.

Such it is with my hometown, a small community that has, for over 300 years, not simply existed as a dot on a map but has been the town so many have called home. An area rich in farmland and inland waterways, the indigenous people, known as the Kuskarawaoks, first settled and flourished here. When the English came to the area, William Penn learned how to speak their language so he could barter and trade with them in order to secure the rights to the area.

In 1681, William Clark received a land grant for the area that would eventually become Harrington. Clark was given a large portion of the lands known as the Mispillion Hundred, a total land grant that encompassed over 3,000 acres of farm and woodland. William's son, Thomas, would later own 650 acres in the center of this vast expanse and build his home here in the early 1700s. He named his piece of heaven "Clark's Folly." It is from this farmhouse our city was born.

The first business was an inn and tavern, constructed by Benjamin Clark, William's grandson, in the late 1700s. He renamed the crossroads Clark's Corner. This location was a major intersection on the stagecoach line linking the ports of Johnnycake Landing, later Frederica, and Milford. With this single building, the stage was set for the city and what would forever be its destiny, where Delaware comes together.

Fast forward to the 1850s and farming had now become the main economic force of Harrington and its surrounding area. Peaches, strawberries, corn, tomatoes, and other sweet fruits and vegetables grew with abundance, but getting these delicate items to market before they would spoil was a challenge. While steamships now traversed the

Delaware River and Delaware Bay daily from local cities to the ports of Philadelphia and Baltimore, a more cost effective and faster method was needed to get these tasty treats to the people of America.

Finally, after years of lobbying and failed attempts, the Delaware Railroad was born. The railroad became the farmers' answer to the transportation issue. Clarks Corner was placed on the line, and for a period of time was the end of the line. Thus, anyone that wanted to ship goods by rail had to come to town. This again made Harrington the place where Delaware came together.

In 1862, Clark's Corner changed its name to Harrington, in honor of Samuel Maxwell Harrington, chancellor of the court in Delaware and the man that had championed the growth of the railroads south. The area around the railroad continued to grow rapidly, and in 1869 the City of Harrington was officially incorporated with the State of Delaware.

"The Hub of Delaware" became Harrington's nickname due to its role on the railroad. As Samuel Harrington predicted, opening Harrington and other areas of Delaware to rail traffic created a boom to all aspects of life. Trains full of freight and passengers traveled the lines multiple times a day. In the 1920s, the next major transportation route was installed. The "DuPont Highway," so named because of its support from Coleman DuPont, ran almost parallel to the railroad, and utilizing the new mode of transportation, the automobile and later trucks, the town took another step forward, but it did come at a cost as well. As in the rest of America, train usage began to decline. The last passenger trains left the area in the 1940s and the freight station closed soon after. Today, the railroad still plays a role in the community, as it serves as a major switching point for rail traffic on the line, but gone is the golden era of the railroad.

Today the city is growing again as it celebrates its sesquicentennial in 2019. To most that live here today, it's still their hometown. People call each other by their first name as they sit down to have coffee in their favorite restaurant. Neighbors still sit outside during a summer night, sharing ice cream and watching the fireflies. The "Mayberry" feel is still very much present in my hometown. While we do not have a mall, a multiplex theater, or a five-star hotel, what we have is home. Small-town America in every way, Norman Rockwell could have made every *Saturday Evening Post* cover from our streets. And to those that made it home so long ago, we owe you a debt of gratitude. You gave us a great place to create our tapestry of home.

ST. STEPHENS CHURCH, FLEMING ST: Originally constructed in 1875, this small unassuming church served until the 1950s as a place of worship for the local Episcopal faithful. The small red church then served as host to the newly formed Harrington Baptist Church until the early 1970s. The building sat abandoned for a few years, forgotten to time. Purchased and gifted to the Greater Harrington Historical Society by John Satterfield, it now beckons proudly to locals and visitors alike, telling not only its story, but the story of Harrington. [*Sepia photo courtesy of the Delaware Public Archives*]

THE FLEMING MANSION, *CIRCA* 1860: Still one of the largest homes ever built in Harrington, Ezekiel Fleming built this nineteen-room mansion in the 1860s after marrying Elizabeth Booth. Fleming's lumber and flour mills were located on the properties next door. Worried that his daughters would get their dresses dirty walking to and from the businesses, he constructed a wooden planked sidewalk just for them. Standing as stately today as it did in the 1860s, the current owners are slowly restoring the home.

JOHN WHITE HOME, LIBERTY STREET, CURRENTLY DELMARVA POWER: Three neighboring homes were constructed in the late 1890s by the same local builder. The homes were even painted the exact same colors. John White, his wife, daughter, Almena, and her son, Frank Rifenburg, resided in one of the houses. The houses were later torn down and Delmarva Power would construct their Harrington office here. Delmarva Power is a direct descendant of the original company that powered Harrington.

GINGERBREAD VICTORIAN HOME ON WEINER AVE: Typical of the homes built in the early 1900s, this home showcased the architectural style so popular in its day. Harrington had several streets lined with this style home, some smaller, as this home shows, and others more grandiose. Shown in a current picture, this home has changed drastically since its early days. As occurred with several homes with open porches, these were later closed in to provide additional living space. [*Sepia photo courtesy of the Delaware Public Archives*]

PRECUT KIT HOME, BUILT IN THE 1910S: Precut homes were a trend starting in the early 1910s. Companies such as Sears and Aladdin Homes sold all the supplies needed to construct your home, except for masonry needs, directly to the consumer. Once ordered, the supplies would be loaded onto two train boxcars and delivered directly to the customer's town for assembly. All the wood, down to the smallest details, were numbered, allowing for the owner to simply hammer them together. Still a residence today, this home shows little change from its original construction.

CORNER OF COMMERCE STREET AND CLARK STREET: Two of the six original streets in Harrington, the area has always been home to the center of the downtown commercial district. Built before the Civil War, these storefronts served a variety of proprietors over their existence. The building on the left once served as the post office for the city. Currently a part of the M & T Banks property, it now serves as an open space within the community.

THE DELAWARE HOUSE, HARRINGTON'S SECOND HOTEL: As the city opened up following the railroad coming to town in 1856, this hotel was built just across from the passenger station. Guests and their luggage would be transported by horse and wagon to the front door of the establishment. When the property was sold, the hotel was divided into three homes and moved to Reese Avenue. The only existing home still shows the obvious connection to the left side of the hotel.

A Religion That Had to Fight the Supreme Court:

St. Paul's African Methodist Church was the last of the eleven AME churches built in Kent County between 1867 and 1895. Established in 1830, it is the oldest documented religious organization in Harrington and has been in practice continuously since that time. The church was organized just seventeen years after the founding of the AME movement by Richard Allen, a former slave and a Delaware resident, before moving to Philadelphia. Pastor Allen successfully sued in 1807 and again in 1815 for the rights of the AME Church to exist independently. After a fire nearly destroyed the church in 1993, it was repaired and serves a thriving congregation today. [*Sepia photo courtesy of the Delaware Public Archives*]

SMALL CHURCH WITH
A STRONG VOICE:
Metropolitan Methodist
Episcopal Church in
Harrington was the second
African American church
founded in the area.
Organized in early 1873 by a
group of trustees headed by
James Friends, the church
was dedicated on October
8, 1893. The church was
extensively remodeled in
the 1920s, and later the
fellowship hall was added
on. The earliest members
would still recognize the
building as it stands today.
[*Sepia photo courtesy of the
Delaware Public Archives*]

THE SCHOOL BELL RINGS: In 1883, the Queen Anne-style school was constructed at a cost of $6,000 and was the first public building constructed by the new city government. By 1910, the number of students had risen to such a high level that the current school had been outgrown. Land was purchased and a new brick school housing first through twelfth grade was constructed on Dorman St., just a block away. Within a few short years, this building too was in need of space, so one of the country one-room schoolhouses, Powell School, was brought to the site and served as the Home Economics classroom. That small school is visible on the left-hand side of the bottom photograph. [*Second photo courtesy of the Delaware Public Archives*]

SCHOOL CONTINUES TO GROW WITH THE CITY: As the community continued to grow, the school's need to house additional students rose as well. In 1928, a wing built to hold an additional 150 students and faculty was constructed. By 1956, another wing was again constructed to house the ever-growing student population. The final construction on this building occurred in 1963 when the original school structure that had been built in 1910 was razed in order to construct W. T. Chipman Junior High School. The last change to this entire complex occurred in 2008, when once again a new school, this time for the elementary grades, was opened. [*Sepia photo courtesy of the Delaware Public Archives*]

COMMERCE STREET IN THE 1920S: This street has witnessed several upgrades since the town was originally laid out in the 1850s. While the streets were still dirt, sidewalks had been upgraded to concrete, the town had electrical power in 1906, and running water had come to town to two years prior. While horse and buggies still traveled the streets in large numbers, cars had become the new favorite mode of transportation. The streetscape has undergone several changes and only a couple of original structures remain still standing. [*Sepia photo courtesy of the Delaware Public Archives*]

EAST SIDE OF COMMERCE ST., 100 YEARS APART: Storefronts lined the east side Commerce Street as you approached Clark Street. Downtown Harrington was home to multiple grocery stores, a druggist, restaurants, and hotels, and the downtown area was a thriving center of commerce. Several of the older structures have been destroyed over the decades. Most of the existing structure shown here were built after the 1930s. [*Sepia photo courtesy of the Delaware Public Archives*]

MECHANIC STREET AFTER THE 1920S: As with many of the original streets in Harrington, oak trees lined both sides of the street. One of the many attractions to Harrington early on was its abundant supply of hardwood trees, which were used for multiple purposes. Once the streets and sidewalks were installed, folks like this young man enjoyed the tree-lined sidewalks for recreation. While a few homes have come and gone, as well as most of the trees, several older homes can still be seen today.

M. P. Church, Harrington, Del.

TRINITY METHODIST CHURCH,
JUNE 6, 1904: Having outgrown their
original small church, a new property
was purchased on Commerce Street, and
the new church was completed later that
year. A large pipe organ was added in
1924, and the Sapp Memorial Building
was added in 1926. The final addition
was the community hall that can be seen
in the color photo. Little else has changed
inside or out of the original structure.

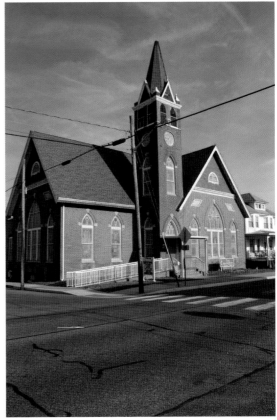

COMMERCE STREET SHOWING THE ORIGINAL BUSINESSES: The Harrington House, the three-story large wood framed structure on the left side of the photo, is the original tavern and inn built by Matthew Clark in the 1850s. The business lasted until the late 1920s, when it was replaced by a new structure. The oldest exiting commercial structure can be seen in the forefront of the photograph. Originally the First National Bank of Harrington, it now is home to the Community Christian Church. [*Sepia photo courtesy of the Delaware Public Archives*]

THE HARRINGTON MILLING COMPANY: Owned by Charles D. Murphy in the 1920s, the Harrington Milling Company was originally constructed by one of Harrington's first entrepreneur's, Ezekiel Fleming. The mill produced flour and cornmeal, which was then transported all over the East Coast by train. Even during the Great Depression, the mill was still very active, producing income of almost $1 million a year. The building remained a mill until the 1980s, at which time it was abandoned and eventually torn down. [*Sepia photos courtesy of the Delaware Public Archives*]

RESIDENTIAL SECTION OF COMMERCE STREET: Just a block removed from the busy commercial section of the town, several large homes were constructed to house the new business families moving into the area. While these homes have undergone various transformations throughout the decades, most are still recognizable today. [*Sepia photo courtesy of the Delaware Public Archives*]

DOCTOR LEWIS HOME: This home was located on the corner of Commerce Street and Mispillion Street. This large Victorian home was commonly called the "House of Seven Gables." The home was well known throughout the city as one of the most beautiful homes in Harrington. After Doctor Lewis' retirement, he moved away and the home was owned by different families until it was razed in the early 2000s, and a new home was constructed.

HARRINGTON MOTORS BUILDING, 100 YEARS APART: Constructed by the Smith family, this Chevrolet dealership was the first and only Chevrolet dealership in town. Lasting from the 1920s to the 1960s, the building was then used by different repair businesses until it became home to True Green Lawn Care. The large neon sign from the Chevrolet dealership can still be seen today at the Greater Harrington Historical Society.

THE JOHN CLYMER HOUSE, DORMAN STREET: Built in the late 1800s for John Clymer and family, this home represents the typical home constructed for the middle class of the day. The home sits just two blocks from the train station. Today the home serves as the community food pantry and has recently been named in honor of Ann Paladino, a longtime volunteer who passed away in 2018.

WEINER AVENUE 100 YEARS APART:
Weiner Avenue was another street
where a large selection of Victorian
homes were built in the late nineteenth
century. Homes such as this one served
as residence to the affluent citizens of
Harrington. The porches played host
to many that sat and watched as the
town grew. Today, as with most of these
homes, the porches have been closed
in to add more living space, but the
Victorian charm remains. [*Sepia photo
courtesy of the Delaware Public Archives*]

THE NEW FIRST NATIONAL BANK OF HARRINGTON, CURRENTLY WSFS: Constructed in 1927, the art deco style building drastically changed the landscape of Harrington. An older wooden structure was demolished to make room for the more modern building; the city's streetscape was changing. The bank printed its own money until 1935. The adjacent store was later demolished to add a drive-through window. Currently serving as home to WSFS, the bank has become an institution in the city.

JACOBS' STORE, PRESENTLY HOME TO BLUE HEN CONSTRUCTION: Standing on the corner of Dorman and Commerce Streets, this wooden structure has played host to some of Harrington's most thriving businesses. The store sold general mercantile goods of the day. After Jacobs store closed, Taylors Hardware expanded into the storefront. Today, it serves the citizens as one of Harrington's most active businesses, and the owner, Darrin Simpson, has an active role within Harrington's Business Association.

PROSPECT METHODIST CHURCH, EAST OF VERNON: Sitting at a small country crossroads about four miles west of Harrington, the present church was constructed in 1874 and dedicated by Bishop Levi Scott. Sunday school rooms were added as needed in 1961, 1967, and 1973 as the church congregation grew. This small but thriving church is still in operation today, and other than the additions, the original structure still stays true to its humble roots. [*Sepia photo courtesy of the Delaware Public Archives*]

DELAWARE BAPTIST UNION CHURCH, 1889: This humble church has undergone major changes since this photograph was taken in 1934. It has also witnessed changes in the groups that have called it home. Built by the Baptist Union, in 1903 it was sold to Harrington Pilgrim Holiness and the Church of the Nazarene. In 1909, a split occurred between these two groups, and the church was turned over to the Pentecostal Church of the Nazarene. It was later sold to the Mount Carmel Seventh-Day Adventist Church, and still serves this congregation today.

First to Current: Built by the VanGesel family as a store, this building also housed the first post office. Then during the 1920s, Denny's Store occupied this site. This business was one of the first stores with home delivery—the truck in the photo could be seen daily making deliveries to local residents. The store was closed in the 1930s and the site was used to construct a new post office. The building was funded using money from President Roosevelt's New Deal. [*Sepia photo courtesy of the Delaware Public Archives*]

RAMSDELL STORE, A FAVORITE FOR LUNCH:
Ramsdell store was located on Center Street, just
one block from the school. Up until the 1960s,
school children could leave school to purchase
their lunch, and with their business so close and
serving what locals called one of the best subs
in town, the store was always busy. Later sold to
Earl Quillen, the storefront was eventually torn
down. Quillen then moved the store to its Dorman
Street location. The property currently sits empty,
awaiting its future occupant.

HEARN OIL COMPANY: This gas station was a part of a Mid Atlantic chain of gas stations that existed in the early 1900s. Located on the newly constructed DuPont Highway, this small station saw many owners over its lifetime. Sold to Sunoco brand in the 1950s, it continued to service locals, switching to Tru Blu, a local brand, until the 1980s. The station sat abandoned for several years until the property was demolished. It now sits open and ready for a new building. [*Sepia photo courtesy of the Delaware Public Archives*]

GAINES ALLEY AND COMMERCE STREET: Showing the town in August 1950, you can see the beehive of activity the town had grown to become. Markets, shops, and the first American Legion Post building are all visible in the busy street. The buildings were home to several storefronts downstairs and both a doctor and dentist office upstairs. Today most of the buildings have been destroyed, but the brick front building still serves small businesses such as Downtown Treasures. [*Sepia photo courtesy of the Delaware Public Archives*]

PUTTING ON THE RITZ: Smith and Raughley was located on Commerce St. in Harrington and sold the finest in men's clothing from the 1920s through the 1940s. It was well known locally that if you wanted to look your best, this was the place to go. The store was on the first floor of the Reese Opera House, Harrington's first full-time movie theater. On May 20, 1916, the Opera House had its most famous guest, Charlie Chaplin, visit. The building played host to the Salvation Army until the early 1980s and was destroyed due to structural issue in the early 2000s. The property has recently been purchased and has begun to undergo redevelopment. [*Sepia photo courtesy of the Delaware Public Archives*]

ANOTHER STOP ON THE RAILROAD: Sitting on the railroad tracks, these two businesses were typical of the expansion in Harrington as a result of the railroad coming south. Supplee-Wills-Jones Milk Company and Atlantic Refining Company took advantage of shipping and receiving goods directly by rail. Today, the site is home to Hudson Farm Supplies. Although the rail siding is gone, you can see the rail bed as it once existed.

EARLY HOME OF HARRINGTON'S GREATEST SHOWMAN: This quaint craftsman style home on Reese Avenue saw the birth and early life of one of Harrington's most influential businessmen and pioneers in the movie theater industry, Reese B Harrington. On the left of the color photo you can even see his first theater. Family members told the story of young Reese showing movies to his friends in the garage and charging for admission. He would also hold a parade with his dog, Champ. Today, the home shows little change from 1910.

AFRICAN AMERICAN SCHOOL IMPROVED: In the 1920s, the DuPont family of Delaware saw the deplorable condition of the African American Schools in Delaware and set out to drastically improve their infrastructure. Schools in many cases, such as the one in Harrington, were removed from their location and completely rebuilt. The early photograph shows the dramatic results: a modern building with students enjoying their new structure. Today the school is gone, but the space is now open athletic fields, allowing all citizens to enjoy the area. [*Sepia photo courtesy of the Delaware Public Archives*]

COMMERCE STREET IN 1930:
The first photograph shows the newly constructed Murphy and Hayes building on the left. The building was constructed by Charles D. Murphy, local entrepreneur, who was involved in many projects. The first floor has always housed businesses ,while the upper floors housed small apartments. Later known as the Quillen Building, today the building still shows little has changed from 1927. [*Sepia photo courtesy of the Delaware Public Archives*]

SANCTUARY FOR METHODISTS: Whites Chapel was located west of Harrington and was the backdrop to the founding of Methodism in America. It was named after Thomas White, judge of the common pleas court in Kent County, Delaware. On March 28, 1778, the Continental Congress ordered Judge White arrested and charged with being a Methodist. White was found innocent. Prior to his arrest, White had received a house guest, Francis Asbury, a missionary from the Methodist Church of England. Both men would remain in seclusion for the rest of the war at Judge White's home. The church fell into disrepair and eventually had to be torn down. Today the cemetery is all that remains of this small chapel and its giant place in history. [*Sepia photo courtesy of the Delaware Public Archives*]

CORNER OF DELAWARE AVENUE AND CENTER STREET: Originally constructed near what was the edge of Harrington and the farms surrounding the city, this home dates to the early 1900s. Today the home has changed little and still sits on its original lot at the corner of Delaware Avenue and Center Street.

MODERN BANKING COMES TO TOWN: The new First National Bank building was constructed in 1927 and at the time of its construction was the most modern building in Harrington, including the first elevator in the city. The original teller windows can be seen here, but now the teller area is located on the opposite of the building after the construction of the drive-through window, which at its time was a first in the area.

P. B. & W. Railroad Depot, Harrington, Del.

THE RAILROAD COMES TO TOWN: The Delaware Railroad came to Clarks Corner in the summer of 1853. The first station was no more than a barn. The second station was constructed in 1886 and later the railroad consolidated with the Philadelphia, Wilmington, and Baltimore Railroads. At its peak in the early 1940s, this station stood witness to as many as twelve passenger trains and twenty freight trains a day. Now serving as the district office for the Delmarva Central Railroad, a division of Carload Express, the station still retains its original look and stands as a silent reminder of the golden days of railroading in the United States.

GAS TO CELLPHONES: Newly constructed in the spring of 1924, this art deco building served as a full-service gas station for decades. Home to Camper's Service Station through the 1950s, it then housed a car parts store, and a second story was added. Remodeled in the late 1990s, the first floor now is home to a cellphone store. [*Sepia photo courtesy of the Delaware Public Archives*]

VICTORIAN HOME ON WEINER AVENUE: Two of the more decorative homes on this street show the influence during the Victorian Era of the Middle and Far East cultures of the world. The unique roof on the tower of these homes was something different and a style not seen anywhere in the small town of Harrington. It is not known, but most believe these homes were built by the same construction company. Both houses and these unique roof lines can still be seen today. [*Sepia photo courtesy of the Delaware Public Archives*]

ONE OF HARRINGTON'S OLDEST FAMILIES BUILDS A HOME: The Wolcott Mansion is one of the oldest homes in the city. It was built in the late 1800s by Henry Clay Wolcott, one of Harrington's first entrepreneurs and a philanthropist. He would later go on to donate property to several churches in the city for their buildings and have a street named in his honor. Today the house is being restored to its former glory.

FURNITURE MAKER TO SCHOOLMARMS: Built by furniture maker and lumberman Omar Franklin in the late 1880s, this stately home again shows off the Victorian architecture so prevalent in Harrington during its initial building boom. The home then became the residence of two of Harrington's great ladies. Heba and Oda Baker were sisters that taught school in Harrington for over eighty years combined. Today, the house is a private multiple-family dwelling.

STUDENTS OF HARRINGTON SCHOOL DISTRICT IN 1923: The State of Delaware had consolidated most of the one-room schoolhouses into local school districts by the late 1920s, following a special report of all schools in the State of Delaware. The report showed poor educational conditions, lacking supplies and teaching curriculums that were not age specific. While the school the photo was taken from has since been torn down, the building of today is still very much alive with the voices and minds of Harrington's youth. [*Sepia photo courtesy of the Delaware Public Archives*]

SHERWIN AND JAILER, NOW THE GENERAL MERCHANDISE STORE, COMMERCE STREET: Constructed just after the turn of the twentieth century, this building was initially used as a dry-cleaning company. However, most remember it as Sherwin and Jailer Shirt Factory. In business until the early 1960s, it then once again became a dry cleaner. The space above the factory was used on Saturday nights for "barn dances" and boxing matches. Today, it has been remodeled and the lower floor serves as a general store called Downtown Junction. The second floor houses a dance studio and apartments.

HOMES ON CLARK STREET 1950 AND TODAY: Santa Claus always came to town. Pulled by a horse, Santa makes his way past the homes built in the 1930s. These homes were built after the Great Depression, which had only minor impacts on this local farming community since they grew most of their own food and the barter system was still alive and well in Harrington at that time. These homes have changed little since their construction.

Swains Hotel Becomes Harrington's First Fast-Food Restaurant: Constructed in the 1930s by Franklin Swain, the hotel served guests from all over the East Coast. Visitors traveling by both train and car would spend the night at what was then the most modern hotel in the area. Closed in the mid-1970s, the building sat on prime real estate and it was only a matter of time before it was torn down and the site would play host to Hardees, opened in the late 1970s as Harrington's first and only fast food restaurant for over ten years. *[Sepia photo Courtesy Hagley Museum & Library]*

DuPont Highway and Milford-Harrington Highway Intersection: Beginning in 1923, and funded by Coleman DuPont, the DuPont Highway was constructed from south to north, providing a new avenue for both commerce and travelers alike throughout the state. Gas stations sprang up to service this new mode of transportation. The intersection has grown, and the flashing traffic signal has been replaced as well. [*Sepia photo courtesy of the Delaware Public Archives*]

PEOPLE'S SERVICE STATION, HARRINGTON'S FIRST 24/7 BUSINESS: Constructed along with the new highway in 1924, People Service Station and Restaurant was opened and quickly became a beehive of activity. Cars, trucks, and buses utilized this travelers beacon for rest, refueling, food, and repairs. The station served as a bus station for Short Line, Red Line, and Greyhound buses. Today, the restaurant now is home to Salty Wave, a seafood establishment, and the Service Station is a tire center. [*Sepia photo courtesy of the Delaware Public Archives*]

TAYLOR & MESSICK, SAME LOCATION EIGHTY YEARS APART: Begun in 1935 by Edward Taylor, Taylor John Deere dealership quickly thrived and grew. By 1940, an old mill was remolded into the storefront seen here. In 1952, Walt Messick came on board to help with the business. Messick purchased the business in the 1960s. Today, his son Jimmy Messick still runs the family business from the same location.

Residential Section of Commerce Street: With the east side of the street still lined by the same trees that existed when the town was founded, the street is now home to some of Harrington's largest homes. The block in the foreground of the street is home to Smith families and their relatives, building almost all the homes in the first block. Today these homes have changed little, and most have been or are currently undergoing restoration.

105 COMMERCE STREET, A. C. CREDICK HOME: Built by a local businessman, A. C. Credick's home was typical of the Arts and Craft-style homes built in the 1920s. Later the home would be sold to George Exley, a local blacksmith. Sadly, George would die young, leaving his wife, Doris, to reside in the home. She would remarry Winston Linton; who later would serve several years as mayor of Harrington. The home today is being remodeled and ready for the next generation that will call Harrington home. [*Sepia photo courtesy of the Delaware Public Archives*]

FROM A SMALL ONE-WINDOW BANK:
The Peoples Bank of Harrington, in
business since 1904, constructed a new
art-deco building in the 1920s. Prior to
this new building, the bank operated
out of a small brick structure that was
only large enough for a single teller
window. The bank remained at this
location until the early 1970s when they
constructed a modern building nearby.
OMG Collage, an antique store, now
resides in the building. [*Sepia photo
courtesy of the Hagley Museum & Library*]

FROM GAS IN YOUR CAR TO INSURANCE FOR YOUR CAR: In the 1940s, Raughley Insurance was remodeled from an older gas station that was on the site. In 1969, the business was sold to Tom Parsons, but kept the Raughley name. Parsons was one of the original founders of the Greater Harrington Historical Society. His office building housed the first museum of the Historical Society. A private office now resides in the building. [*Sepia photo courtesy of the Hagley Museum & Library*]

STONES HOTEL NINETY YEARS APART: Stone's Hotel has long been known to locals as the tavern most went to for a sandwich, pizza, and a beer. Some Friday and Saturday nights the business would be so busy, people could barely enter the bar. The hotel rooms were long-term rent rooms for railroad men and other travelers. Nearly destroyed by fire in 2015, the business has reopened, and its famous pizza can once again be enjoyed by all. [*Sepia photo courtesy of the Hagley Museum & Library*]

HARRINGTON FIRE COMPANY TO HARRINGTON POLICE STATION: Constructed in the 1930s, the fire station was home to the men, and later women, of the Harrington Fire Company, an all-volunteer organization, providing fire and EMS care to the citizens and visitors of Harrington. Once the fire company built a new station in July of 2000, the city purchased the building and remolded the structure to become home of the Harrington Police Department. [*Sepia photo courtesy of the Delaware Public Archives*]

FLEMING STREET, ONE OF THE ORIGINAL SIX IN THE CITY: Now lined with homes from various eras, Fleming Street is now a hub of activity in the 1940s. Constructed as one of Harrington's six original streets, it was lined with houses spanning several decades of building. The home in the right foreground now serves as the Harrington Senior Center. The house in the left foreground, now gone, was home to Dr. Hewitt Smith. His wife, Martha, volunteered to drive the city fire trucks during World War II to help with the manpower shortage. [*Sepia photo courtesy of the Delaware Public Archives*]

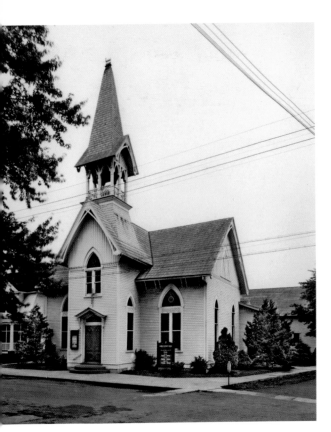

ASBURY CHURCH, OVER 120 YEARS OLD: Constructed first in 1870, the church was rebuilt in 1890. In 1915, the church had a beautiful pipe organ installed with the financial help of Andrew Carnegie. The church then added a fellowship hall and church school rooms to serve the growing population. Today, the church still serves the community faithful. [*Sepia photo courtesy of the Delaware Public Archives*]

PENSUPREME ICE CREAM CLARK STREET: A branch of Penn Dairies, Pensupreme Ice Cream quickly became a favorite of locals and travelers alike. Harrington citizens had a sweet tooth, as there were at any one time four or more ice cream parlors. A restaurant would later be added to feed the local citizens. The inside has since been remodeled and now is an auto body shop, but one of the original signs still hangs on the front of the building, reminding locals of the past and the sweet memories from long ago. [*Sepia photo courtesy of the Delaware Public Archives*]

THE SECOND DAIRY TO OPEN IN HARRINGTON: Hi-Grade Dairy was constructed in the 1930s and grew quickly to a local favorite. With a large supply of fresh milk from the local dairy farms, the plant had no shortage of raw ingredients. Benny Hughes was the owner during the 1950s and added a small lunch counter that served homemade ice cream, which locals ate by the gallon. Blue Hen Foods Packing is the latest business to reside in the building and produces organic granola bars for schools.

CKRT POST #7 AMERICAN LEGION: The Callaway, Kemp, Raughley, Tee American Legion post was founded in October of 1919 and later named after these four men, all of whom were killed in action during World War II. The building was constructed in 1948 and served as the organizations home for the next fifty-plus years. After building a new post home, the property sat abandoned until 2019, when Taco Bell constructed a restaurant.

MILFORD HARRINGTON HIGHWAY EAST OF TOWN LOOKING WEST: With the advent of cars and trucks, the newly completed highway expanded the city eastward. Homes and businesses were quick to build near this newly completed road network. Construction even continues today. The highway was later made into a divided highway for increased traffic. Midway Shopping Center opened in the late 1990s and Holiday Inn Express opened the same decade—all show the continued importance of this vital highway. [*Sepia photo courtesy of the Delaware Public Archives*]

CUPIDS ICE CREAM TO DOWNHOME DIXIE: Owned by Jesse Porter of Greensboro, Maryland, the small ice cream store was a favorite of locals and visitors alike, serving hand dipped ice cream that was produced by Porter's plant in Greensboro. Employees say the store was so popular in the summer that on weekends it was not uncommon to close after midnight. Later, the building became home to a staple of Harrington, the *Harrington Journal*, now owned by Harry Farrow. After the paper closed, the building sat vacant. It has been restored by Blue Hen Construction and today is the location of Downhome Dixie, a vintage furniture store.

J R KATES GROCERY AND PETER PAN GIFT SHOP: Owned by Reynolds Kates and located on Commerce Street, Kates Grocery Store was one of the many general stores carrying a variety of groceries and other sundries. On the left was Peter Pan's Gift Shop, with Mrs. Ethel Reed as the shop's proprietor. Selling gifts, card, and candy, Commerce Street was commonly called Candy Lane due to the number of candy stores located in the area. The next building to occupy this lot was the Harrington Public Library. Now the area is home to Staples Insurance.

"BIGGER AND BETTER": Beginning as the Kent and Sussex Fair in 1920, the aerial view from the 1920s shows an already active event. The fair was begun to celebrate the agriculture of Delaware. Today the fairgrounds have grown to over 300 acres and attendance figures routinely exceed 250,000 people a year. In 2019, the Delaware State Fair will be celebrating its 100th birthday. [*Sepia photo courtesy of Hagley Museum & Library] [Color photo courtesy of the Delaware State Fair*]

KENT & SUSSEX FAIR MIDWAY 1950s TO TODAY: With guest numbers now over 100,000 for the week-long event, the fair had become a huge draw and economic boost for the city, with performers such as the famous Radio City Music Hall Rockettes, singers Frankie Avalon, Pat Boone, and even an appearance by the Lone Ranger. Today the carnival grounds are as popular as ever, lighting up the night sky as over 200,000 people annually visit the now ten-day event.

THE FAIR SIDESHOWS: The sideshow tents were very popular with fair goers each year. Made popular in America by P. T. Barnum, soon every carnival had its own version of this attraction. From the sword swallower, the human block head and various strange and unique animals, patrons would pay 10 cents to see the oddities of the sideshow. The "girlie shows" were also a part of these traveling caravans—ladies would dance in an adults-only show. Today the sideshow has changed but they are still attracting people to stare at the unusual and odd.

CARNIVAL GAMES AND FOOD HAVE CHANGED LITTLE: Everyone has enjoyed games of chance at the fair. Pitching pennies for "carnival" glass, knocking over stuffed animals to win a prize, or shooting clay pipes, visitors to the fair would flock to these games to try their luck and win a prize. While the games have become more modern, guys still try to win a prize for their favorite gal. [*Sepia photo courtesy of the Delaware Public Archives*]

FAIR FOOD ALWAYS TASTES BETTER: While the sights and sounds of the fair are favorites, nothing draws more people than the smell of food cooking. Whether it's fried, grilled, sweet, or a combination of several items, the food stands always draw a crowd. Each has their favorite fair food or sugary treat. In 100 years, that has not changed and probably never well. [*Sepia photo courtesy of the Delaware Public Archives*]

FARMING HAS ALWAYS BEEN THE FOCUS: The Kent and Sussex Fair was stared to celebrate agriculture in the area. Farm machinery dealers from around Delmarva would bring their new machinery to the fair, looking to entice a farmer to purchase a new tractor, harvester, plow, or seeder. Today's farm machinery area is still a fair favorite for many. [*Sepia photo courtesy of the Delaware Public Archives*]

THE RISE OF HARNESS RACING IN HARRINGTON: The new harness paddock was constructed at the Harrington Raceway in 1946. Harness racing had always been a staple of the fair since it opened, but with the birth of pari-mutuel wagering, the new building was needed. Later, as the sport grew, a new paddock and office complex were constructed. The harness track has played host to some of the world's fastest and most famous harness racing horses including: Adios Harry, Rainbow Blue, and Shartin N., our newest millionaire horse in Delaware. [*Sepia photo courtesy of the Delaware Public Archives*]

FROM HARNESS RACING TO SLOTS MACHINES: Harness racing had become such a show that special dates of racing were created and admission was charged. Over a thousand people would daily pack the grandstands to see these magnificent animals run. While today's grandstand crowds are never that large, casino gambling helped pump money and life back into a dying industry. Harrington Raceway and Casino now entertains locals and visitors with table games, slots, dining, and entertainment. [*Sepia photo courtesy of the Delaware Public Archives*]

COMMUNITY SERVICE FOR CLOSE TO 100 YEARS: The New Century Club purchased this building on Dorman Street in 1921. The group's mission is to improve their town with projects for the citizens and beautification of the city streets through the use of trees and flower beds. The building is now owned by the city and is named in honor of former mayor Robert Price. [*Sepia photo courtesy of the Delaware Public Archives*]

HARRINGTON SHIRT FACTORY BECOMES ENVIROCORP: After World War II, Harrington became home to multiple garment factories. Bolts of fabric would come to town by train or truck, cut and made into shirts, and the goods would then be shipped back to the major cities. The company made uniform shirts, as well as shirts for high-end retailers such as Sacks Fifth Avenue. After closing, the building sat vacant until a native son, Joe Gannon, redeveloped the space to house his business, Envirocorp. The business specializes in the testing of water and other chemical analysis.

ACE DRESS COMPANY, S. DUPONT HIGHWAY: Perhaps the largest of the garment companies in Harrington, Ace Dress Company produced some of the finest dresses in the United States. Sold in some of America's high-end boutiques and department stores such as Macy's and Gimbels, these garments would be the fashion trend of the year. Amazing to think these rural ladies in the small town of Harrington were producing the country's latest fashions. Here, striking for better wages, these ladies were led by a little spitfire named Ethel Reed, fourth from the right. Her reputation is well known to this author because she is my grandmother. Today, the building is property of American Finance and is being remodeled for future use.

Pat Fry's Amoco Station becomes Sylvester Custom Cabinetry: Opened after returning from the war, Fry's Amoco was located on the northbound lanes of DuPont Highway. Serving town folks and travelers alike, Fry's Amoco was one of the busiest stations in town. Now repurposed, local custom cabinet maker Greg Sylvester owns the space and operates his cabinet manufacturing operation and business office here.

OLD SCHOOL REUSED TO BECOME A HOUSE: With over thirteen one-room schoolhouses now sitting abandoned due to the consolidation of these schools, citizens looked for many uses of these buildings. Some became barns, others chicken houses, and a few were turned into houses. This house was the original African-American school in the city. Sitting on Milby Street today, you can still see the one-room schoolhouse on the right side.

ST. BERNADETTE' CATHOLIC CHURCH, SIXTY YEARS OF SERVICE: In 1954, this beautiful stone building was constructed, except for the roof rafters, completely by the church members. Taking almost two years to complete, it gave those of the Catholic faith a church to call home. Prior to this, they had rented different businesses and schools to hold services. The church has since added a parish hall and Sunday school building. The church itself shows little change since its initial construction.

INDIVIDUAL SHOPS, CAHALL AND SHAW, L & D ELECTRONICS TO CLUTTER BOX: The only currently existing set of row shops that were constructed just after the 1900s, this row of buildings has seen multiple tenants and changes to their construction in over 100 years. Initially built as three separate buildings, the shops were combined to make Cahall and Shaw Furniture in the 1940s. This was the first large scale retailer in the city. Later home to L & D Electronics, a television sales and repair shop, today it plays host to the Clutter Box Antique shop.

QUILLEN'S SHOPPING CENTER CHANGES THE CITY: Harrington's first strip mall was constructed in the 1950s and forever changed the downtown landscape. With the only large supermarket moving in, as well as now the only existing pharmacy in town, the downtown business area lost two of its anchor stores. Slowly, over the next decades, more and more stores followed this example and left the downtown area. Today the entire complex has been rented to Connections, an addiction rehabilitation center. [*Sepia photo courtesy of the Delaware Public Archives*]

REESE THEATER, SMALL THEATER WITH A HUGE IMPACT: Reese Harrington has already been mentioned in this book as an entertainer from an early age. The first building on this location opened on March 2, 1922. After a fire destroyed the building in 1943, the theater reopened to great fanfare on October 4, 1945. Harrington was known all over the East Coast as a visionary. He was the first to show a 3D movie in Delaware, constantly improving sound, movie screens, and the entire theater experience. After closing in 1965, the building was sold to Peoples Bank, who constructed a new facility. The bank today is home to M&T Bank. [*Sepia photo courtesy of the Delaware Public Archives*]

HUMBLE ESSO, A TOUCH OF THE SOUTHWEST: Constructed in the late 1940s, the Humble gas station was an example of the craze that swept the country of using the clay tile roof line so popular in the American Southwest area. While a unique look in Harrington, the business itself was not as successful. The building has been host to numerous vehicle repair businesses over the years—today the Harrington Motor World used car lot resides at the location. Through all the building's residents, the one-of-a-kind roof line has always been this building's trademark. [*Sepia photo courtesy of the Delaware Public Archives*]

HORSEPOWER IN SEVERAL WAYS: Blue Hen Racing was a local small clay dirt track, located just south of Harrington. Begun by a small group of local men, the group began with each man putting up ten dollars. At its peak, the track had racers from all over the Mid-Atlantic region and saw over 100 entries for each race day. After the closing of the raceway, the land sat vacant until another group specializing in horsepower constructed their business. Today, Chick's Saddlery, a business specializing in horse equipment and Western clothing, calls the former raceway home.

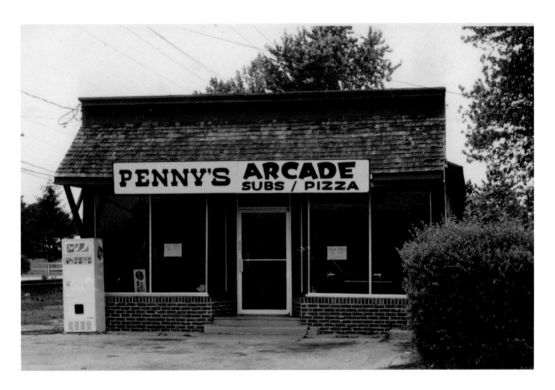

SAM SHORT, STORE OWNER AND
SO MUCH MORE: In the 1950s, Sam
Short owned a small convenience
store on Center Street in Harrington.
Non-descript as most general stores of
the time, Sam's store held a secret in the
back room. His store played host to Blue
Hen Records, a rockabilly label that saw
moderate success. Later the store became
an arcade and pizza restaurant. Today a
family home sits on the site. I wonder if
they can still hear the music.

Burton's to Main Street Café: Every town has its icons. Burton's Sport Shop is a name that evokes a smile from anyone born in Harrington before 1980. Owned by Burton and Alma Smith in 1934, Burton's was to many the place their youth. Fountain Soda, ice cream floats, subs, and the famous peas and dumpling soup may have been the menu staples, but the sights, sounds, and smells are what left an impression on so many. Today, a new group of memories are made at Main Street Café, a local restaurant that still invites Harrington's locals to sit, have coffee, and chat about yesterday and today.

WHEELER'S PARK, HARRINGTON'S ANSWER TO DISNEY: Begun in 1947 and lasting until 1978, Wheeler's Park was small, had a few pieces of playground equipment, a small pool, a stream, monkeys, and a train. And to every kid around, it was a wonderland—a place that for ten cents, you could spend an entire summer day with your friends. Laughing and playing, William Wheeler, the owner and proprietary, would be right there with you, yelling the loudest as the small train went through the concrete tunnel. The bandstand was one of the center pieces in the park. It still sits today, awaiting the next musicians to come play.

THE WISHING WELL AT WHEELER'S PARK: Everyone has wishes. And for a penny dropped in the wishing well you could hope one day your dreams would come true. As if frozen by time, the wishing well still awaits its next coin, its next wish to be made. Hopefully one day, the park will return in some form and the wish most locals have, a park for the community, will come true.

CALLIS-THOMPSON INCORPORATED, THE BACKBONE OF MODERN TRAVEL: Opened in the 1950s by George Thompson, the company was a regional leader in supplying America's growing need for gasoline. The company installed underground tanks, pumps, and delivery trucks for all types of petroleum products. Chances are if you fueled up a vehicle on the East Coast in the late twentieth century, you did so using their equipment. Today, the company is gone but the building remains as a reminder of this small city's role in the growth of the automotive love affair in America.

HI-GRADE, BENNY'S JUNCTION AND NOW ROYAL FARMS: Hi-Grade Restaurant had grown in such popularity by the 1970s that its owner, Benny Hughes, decided to open a restaurant and ice cream parlor. Growing ever busier still, and noticing a need for a "good place to eat good food" as he would say, Hughes would later rebrand the restaurant to Benny's Junction. It served a specialty of steaks and other foods, all while a small toy train rolled overhead to keep the train theme going that the restaurant chose as its branding. After closing in early 2000s, the property was purchased by Royal Farms of Baltimore and a convenience store was constructed on the site.

BURRIS FOODS BECOMES THE CITY'S LARGEST EMPLOYER: Burris Logistics, or as it was known then, Burris Foods, started in 1925 when John W. Burris and his father, Edward, began delivering tomatoes from the farms in lower Delaware and Maryland to markets in Philadelphia. On the return trips, they delivered freshly baked bread to Acme Markets. In 1973, looking to expand, the company constructed a frozen food distribution facility in Harrington. It has since tripled in size and now is the largest employer in the area. The Burris brand is now national, serving all fifty states from over sixteen locations across the country.

WESLEY METHODIST CHURCH: Located in Burrsville, the church served the small farms and families of faith that existed far outside of Harrington. Constructed in 1834, the church served both citizens from Delaware and Maryland since it stood just feet away from the state line. The second, pictures here, was constructed in 1872. After being destroyed by fire in 1934, a new church was built inside of a year and ready for Christmas service in December of 1934. This small church continues its service today as the Union United Methodist Church.

ACKNOWLEDGMENTS

I have to start by thanking everyone that has believed in me and stood by me. Without the support of so many, I would not be who I am today.

To my wife and proofreader, Lisa, thank you for helping me keep the ice salesman's pitch to the Eskimos short.

To my children. My sweet daughter Vickie for putting up with dad as I took over the family room for this project. My son Brian, a feather when I needed one, a song to brighten my heart, I know you have my back.

To the matriarch of Harrington, Charlotte Hutson. Not just my aunt, but my source of local history.

To the staff at Fonthill, specifically my editor Kena, thank you for keeping me on the straight and narrow, a tough task by only email and phone calls.

To the Greater Harrington Historical Society for entrusting me with not only the photographs for this project, but for allowing me to tell the stories of all of us that have ever called Harrington home.

And finally, to all who pick up this book and open its pages: as with our city, your story isn't finished. It may not have even been written yet. So, go out a make it an adventure. Remember, a caterpillar once could not fly either, but now has beautiful wings.